Better Trampolining

ROY DAVIS and ALAN MACDONALD

Better Trampolining

Kaye & Ward · London

First published in Great Britain by
Kaye & Ward Ltd
21 New Street, London EC2M 4NT
1980

ISBN 0 7182 1467 6

Printed in Great Britain by Whitstable Litho Ltd, Whitstable, Kent

Contents

Foreword

It gives me pleasure to have been asked to introduce this book on trampolining by Roy Davis and Alan Macdonald.

The book is not intended as an instruction manual for those people who have achieved some success in the sport, but rather as an introduction and guide to the beginner, whether they be coach or performer. The key points for many of the basic skills from the tuck jump progressing through to the Barani, are clearly stated in an easy to follow manner.

The book emphasizes the constant need for safety awareness, and who better to state the case than someone, like Roy, who has suffered a very serious injury when trampolining. The need for would-be trampoline coaches to attend approved qualification courses is also emphasized and the British Trampoline Federation (B.T.F.) with its highly structured Coaching Development Scheme would endorse these recommendations.

There will, of course, be disagreement on some of the points mentioned, and it's right that there should be, for what better stimulus is there for us to review our teaching methods and coaching practices. However, no pretentious claims are made by the authors but rather an honest review of the techniques and progressions they have found to be most helpful in practice. For this reason the book should be included in every school reference library.

As Secretary to the Yorkshire and North Midlands Division of the B.T.F. I am pleased to commend this book to all who are interested in trampolining, whether they are teachers, performers, or even enthusiastic parents. There is something in it for everyone. In doing this I would also like to congratulate Roy and Alan on its production and give them a special thanks from all those would-be coaches or aspiring performers who no doubt will find it helpful, stimulating and thought provoking.

John Duffy.

Introduction

Trampolining is a young sport which was developed in the late 1930's, and involved tumbling and twisting tricks very similar to high and springboard diving. The primary difference between the two sports is that in trampolining, take off and landing can be executed in any one of a number of different positions, e.g. from the back, knees, chest and feet.

Many years elapsed from the conception of the trampoline to the time when the first world championships were held in 1964, and during those years the equipment was widely used as a training aid for divers. With a trampoline, they could train consistently and intensively, and thus eliminate the tiresome aspect of their own sport, of becoming wet and cold between dives.

One particular diver, who was quick to realise the training potential of the trampoline was Brian Phelps, who was an Olympic diving medallist, and eventually became a member of the British Trampoline team.

The trampoline has become a part of the equipment of many hospitals and special schools, since its uses are beneficial to physiotherapy in developing timing, co-ordination, and bodily fitness. As a sport in its own right it involves excitement, skill, and courage, and the end results are exhilarating and beautiful to watch.

In this book we will try to explain, in layman's language, some of the more important aspects of the sport.

1. Safety.
2. Types of Equipment.
3. Performing.
4. Competing.

It is necessary to point out at this stage that the opinions expressed here, are only intended as a guide to the reader. The methods of teaching and hand spotting, described and photographed, are those which we have found to work best for ourselves. Individual teachers will find their own system by experimenting and adaptation. Coaches should always question teaching methods and look for improvements. In this way the sport will advance rather than stagnate. We believe that would-be teachers of this sport should attend a B.T.F. coaching course.

1. Safety in Trampolining

Safety must be the key word in trampolining. If you are proposing to adopt the sport, please do not by-pass this section, but read it thoroughly. It is of paramount importance, even to the most experienced of performers.

The life of a performer may depend upon him observing the proper code of conduct on the trampoline. Regardless of experience, read this section thoroughly and refresh your memory.

It is assumed that the reader will, or does, attend trampoline sessions conducted by a qualified coach, therefore it is also assumed that the teacher will take all relevant safety precautions. The performer should, however, try to help by taking the following precautions for himself.

1. He must never attempt to erect a trampoline unless his coach directly instructs him to do so. The equipment is often heavy and awkward to assemble, so here the experience and training of the instructor are invaluable.

2. The pupil should wear suitable clothing to protect his knees and elbows from grazes, which could be inflicted by the webbing of the bed. Track suits are ideal for this purpose. Where ever possible he must also wear a pair of proper trampolining slippers with rubber soles. Suede soled gym. shoes are not good for trampolining. Trampoliners must not bounce in bare feet.

3. For basic reasons, bracelets, necklaces, rings, watches etc. must not be worn while the performer is attending a trampoline session. These items could cause an accident to coach, performer, or spotter*. Pupils must ensure that their finger nails are short, and girls in particular must see that long hair is securely tied back, in order that performances are not inhibited by a shower of hair.

*Performers who guard the sides of the trampoline to prevent accidents by falling.

4. Pupils should never disagree with their coach, since he will always have a good reason for a decision, and their safety and progress will always be uppermost in his mind.

5. Performers must, under no circumstances, attempt to organise their own trampolining sessions without the guidance of a coach. Apart from reasons of safety they are usually not insured if they are unsupervised.

6. The human body is not a machine, and must be treated with respect. If a body is tired, and is asked to exert itself, coordination suffers and accidents occur. Bounce in short bursts rather than for long periods. (30 to 45 seconds is sufficient for each attempt).

7. Performers may be tempted to show off and try to exceed their own limits, this again could lead to accidents.

8. Always warm up at the beginning of a session by performing some simple skills, such as tucks, pikes, and pike straddles. This loosens up the performer and helps him to become used to the equipment.

The trampoline is an innocent piece of equipment, which, if not used safely and correctly, may appear as a savage beast waiting for some unsuspecting prey to come along. Even the most competent performer may fall into its trap. It waits for a performer to forget a safety rule then attacks, and like all savage beasts it shows no mercy.

1. **Spotting stance.** Adopt a balanced position with the legs well spaced apart. Do not cross the legs. Always watch the performer.

Spotting a falling body. (2. and 3.)   2
2. Stand your ground, and push the performer back onto the equipment.

3. When a performer is falling off, try to lower him to the ground, if possible without holding a limb.

3

2. Types of Equipment

A trampoline is a piece of gymnastic equipment consisting of a flexible nylon bed, attached by springs to a tubular steel frame. The designs of the trampoline are many and varied, each with its own advantages. The equipment comes in two basic forms:

(a) **Floor Models** are usually built from tubular steel sections, which are hinged and collapsible. They are fitted with roller stands and consequently are fully portable. Each one, of a variety of sizes, has a particular use.

   Nissen Trampolines Ltd. make two very popular types, the 77A and the Goliath. The 77A is useful since it is of a convenient size for swing time routines, and is relatively inexpensive. The Goliath is significantly larger, and therefore allows the performer more space in which to work.

(b) **Pit Models** are situated permanently in one place. They are rectangular steel frames fitted with springs and beds. The whole structure is sited over a pit in the floor or ground. They are obviously not portable and the pits tend to become convenient large waste paper bins!

Springs come in two varieties:

(a) **Elastic.** These are not as powerful as steel springs, but are completely quiet and safe.

(b) **Steel.** These tend to be rather noisy, but provide a good balanced recoil, and so are of more use to the good performer since they are capable of giving him greater height when executing difficult moves.

Beds can be of the following varieties:

(a) **Mesh** — made up of interwoven strips of nylon, whose regular pattern of holes allows air to pass through the structure during bouncing. The reduced air resistance allows a sharper recoil, and consequently gives more power. The narrower the webbing – the more powerful the equipment.

(b) **Full (Solid) Beds,** were the first beds ever used on the trampoline and are very sluggish to bounce on. The absence of holes in the bed means that

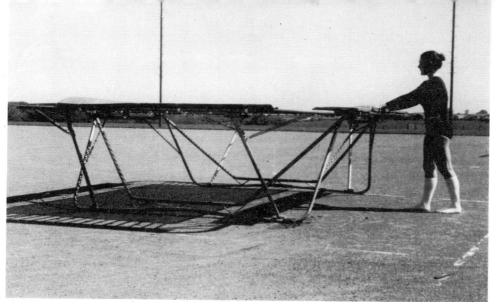

4. Nissen 77A trampoline.

air cannot pass through, and recoil is therefore very slow. These beds are of value to toddlers who cannot see the floor through them, and may have a greater sense of security.

Ideal Trampoline

Schools and sports centres etc. proposing to purchase trampolines may seek advice from the B.T.F. regional secretaries who will be glad to suggest the best combination of equipment to satisfy the needs of the particular organisation.

5. Beginners may prefer to start by wearing a safety harness.

3.   Performing

Free Bouncing

The act of simply bouncing up and down on a trampoline is known as *free bouncing*. Before any skill can be attempted, a performer must learn how to bounce safely and properly, without travelling over the trampoline bed. This is best done in the following manner.

Stand, feet slightly apart, in the centre of the trampoline where the two red lines cross. Face the end of the apparatus, and focus the eyes on the blue-green crash pad which covers the steel frame.

Gently push the feet into the bed by flexing the knees. This will make the bed recoil and push the performer into the air. As he leaves the bed, the performer should reach forwards and upwards with his arms. This action should lift the body straight up from the bed.

As the body returns to the bed the arms should be brought smoothly down to the sides, ready to repeat the lifting action on the next bounce.

It is important that the arms are at no time brought behind the body, since this causes a loss of balance and the performer tends to fall.

The key to successful bouncing is a smooth rhythm. The performer should try to be fluent and cut any jerkiness out of his movements.

The adoption of a fairly wide stance before bringing the feet together in the air aids balance. Later on performers will learn to bounce with their feet almost together as they develop their technique. Beginners must learn to control a low bounce before they can inspect the ceiling at close quarters!

Experienced performers must know how and when to use the bounce, both before and between exercises.

6

7

Free bouncing. (6. -8.) Stretch head and chest up for a straight position in the air. On landing bend the knees to stop.

8

Check Bouncing

This is the act of stopping bouncing completely within the space of one bounce. It is accomplished by bending the knees slightly as the performer hits the bed, so absorbing its recoil.

Inexperienced performers should avoid bending the knees too much since there comes a point when if a joint is overflexed the performer will lose balance and control, and perhaps injure himself.

Any new performer must practise until he can stop immediately at any time. He must also practise straight bouncing in order to cultivate good controlled flight, height and control. Performers with tension in their muscles bounce more efficiently than do those who are relaxed.

9. **Check bouncing.** Bend the knees on landing to stop.

18

Tucked Jump

The apparent simplicity of this exercise belies both its difficulty and its importance.

The trick is performed by folding the knees into the chest, at the top of the bounce, touching them for a split second with the hands, letting them go and extending the legs and landing on the feet.

It is important that on take off the performer stretches upwards, and tries to time the move so that it happens exactly at the top of the bounce. Always try to make this a quick, smooth exercise, and avoid holding onto the knees for a long time, or tucking too soon.

Tucked jump. (10. and 11.) Stretch up at take off. The performer's hands must make contact with the leg, just below the knees.

10   11

Piked and Piked Straddle Jumps

These are both very closely related to the tuck jump, and are phased in exactly the same way. The take off and point of execution of these two exercises are identical to those of the tucked jump.

Piked Jump

Here the performer lifts and extends his legs, keeping them pressed together with toes pointed. To complete the move, the performer reaches for his ankles with his hands and immediately reverts to a standing position to return to the bed.

Piked jump. (12. and 13.) Stretch up at take off. Pike at the top of the bounce.

12   13

Piked Straddle Jump

The leg position and hand position are identical to the piked jump, except that the legs are stretched as wide as possible for a moment then closed and extended downwards before landing.

The importance of these skills cannot be overestimated. They are usually the first to be learned, and must be performed well before anything more advanced can be attempted. This is because they are aerial tricks and serve as good training in developing height, control, timing and balance. Tucks and pikes are particularly valuable since they form the middle phases of many advanced skills such as somersaults.

These three skills are also useful to any aspiring performer in grade three competitions, for although their tariff value is 0.0 they fit nicely into routines between more difficult stunts, so allowing performers to regain their balance and composure between difficult skills.

Piked straddle jump. (14. and 15.) Stretch up at take off. Straddle at the top of the bounce.

14

15

On attempting these exercises for the first time, performers will be counted through by their coach. Until he is satisfied that the exercise is performed safely the coach may step onto the bed and support the performer's landing.

Useful Exercise

When these skills have been mastered a good exercise is to learn to string them together in swing time, which means performing them one after the other in consecutive bounces, taking off from and landing on the same spot on the bed and using consistent height.

22

Knee Drop

This skill involves a different landing position and is quite simple to perform. As for all exercises, the take off should be straight upwards stretching for the ceiling, and when the performer has reached the top of his bounce he should merely fold his knees into a kneeling position. He should land on the bed with his feet together and his knees slightly apart. The performer should keep his back STRAIGHT throughout the execution of this skill.

The balance of this exercise is critical. If the pupil's back is not straight then he is likely to travel, collapse, or even somersault. The performer should push his knees into the bed on landing, and reach up with his arms for a controlled return to feet.

Knee drop. (16.-18.)

16. Stretch up on take off.

17. Adopt the knee drop position in the air with straight back.

18. Land with a straight back, looking at the end of the bed, ready to stretch up to feet.

Half Twist Jump

This skill is performed in the air, though like all basic twists it is created whilst the feet are still in contact with the bed. It is obviously important to learn the half twist, since it forms either the basis or the main part of many tumbling and twisting tricks. The half twist is worth 0.1 in tariff value and is most useful as a balancing trick in grade three competitions.

To execute it the performer should:

1. Bounce with his eyes focussed on an end of the trampoline.
2. At take off he should stretch up with both arms, making his body

24

position both straight and vertical, whilst creating a slight turn with head and shoulders.

3.   When he believes himself to be at the top of his bounce, the pupil should be facing the opposite end of the trampoline.

Full Twist

Is merely an extension of the half twist. The take off and point of execution are both identical to the previous skill, but instead of stopping at half twist the head looks round for the end of the trampoline which the performer was facing at take off.

Arm positions are important and can vary from a horizontal to a vertical position depending upon such factors as the amount of twist, eg. half, full, one and a half, double etc. or the height at which they are to be performed. Twists must be completed whilst in the air.

Half and full twists.
(19.-22.)

19. Stretch up at take off and begin the twist.

20. One third of the way round, looking for the end of the trampoline.

21. Two thirds of the way round.

26

22. The twist complete.

Seat Drop

This is regarded as one of the basic landings in trampolining. It is a valuable skill since it lends itself to a range of more advanced skills. It is also useful to the new performer because it is probably the first exercise which he will learn which involves a landing position other than the feet. The fact that it involves dropping onto the bottom and pushing back onto the feet makes this an impressive move to the beginner.

The correct position for the seat drop can be learned by sitting on the floor, legs tight together, straight ahead and toes pointed. The performer should lean slightly backwards with the hands behind the back and in contact with the floor, fingers pointing forwards. The finger positions are important for safety reasons.

To learn the seat drop on the trampoline, it is advisable to attempt the exercise from one low bounce, gently pushing the hips slightly forwards when at the top of the bounce. The legs are then pushed forwards following the centre line of the bed during the descent in order to achieve the correct landing position on the bed.

Once the performer has become more experienced he may concentrate on reaching upwards with his arms and chest at take off. He should leave his legs extended down towards the bed, until he has begun to drop back towards the bed. Adopting the seat drop position on the descent gives better balance and control.

The standing position is regained after the move by pushing hard with the hands on landing and stretching the arms upwards.

Seat drop. (23.-26.)
23. Stretch up at take off and lean slightly backwards.

24. Move into a good landing position.

25. Seat drop landing position.

26. After landing
stretch up, and land
on the feet.

Swivel Hips (Seat drop, half twist to seat drop)

This is a very stylish exercise which the newcomer to the sport can learn, and perform without much difficulty. It is therefore a trick which gives great satisfaction, but its use competitively is limited because its tariff value is only 0.1, and the skill involves more than one contact with the bed.

   Before the performer can reasonably try the swivel hips he must be able to perform the seat drop and half twist in a competent fashion.
Progressions to learning the swivel hips:
1.   The performer must first learn to land the seat drop with his legs absolutely straight and with his toes pointed. A good hard push from the hands as the performer hits the bed will be sufficient to make him stand up again. Stretching the arms upwards when leaving the bed will also help to regain the standing position.
2.   The next step towards completing the trick is to convert the seat drop into a seat drop with half twist to a standing position. This is accomplished

30

by lifting quickly from the seat drop position, beginning the twist while in contact with the bed and when the body is completely vertical, spinning the head round to face the opposite end of the trampoline, so causing the whole body to twist.

3. Once this move has been mastered the pupil must perform his seat drop half twist to standing, bounce once and then perform another seat drop.

4. The complete exercise may then be attempted by (a) ensuring a good high lift from the bed, (b) driving the feet backwards and twisting into another seat drop.

Faults

A very common fault with this trick is that performers do not actively drive their feet underneath their bodies but try to swing them around the side to the second seat drop, while their bodies are still in the first seat drop position.

It should be emphasised that the legs and feet must be straight and driven underneath the trunk of the body, while this skill is being performed.

Build up sequence to this trick

1. Seat drop.
2. Seat drop, half twist to stand.
3. Seat drop, half twist to stand, bounce, seat drop.
4. Seat drop, half twist to seat drop, (swivel hips).

Alternative method of teaching.

1. Seat drop.
2. Seat drop, half twist to stand.
3. Half twist to seat drop.
4. Seat drop, half twist to seat drop, (swivel hips).

Swivel hips. (27.-31.)
Normal seat drop, stretch up and begin twisting whilst still in contact with the bed. Whilst twisting look at the end of the bed for as long as possible. This will help lift, and twist. Lean back slightly on landing the second seat drop, then stretch back up to feet.

28

29

32

30

31

Hands and Knees Drop

The importance of this exercise is not as a move in its own right, but as a significant intermediate stage in the learning of other skills.

The correct position for the hands and knees drop can be adopted on the floor, by crouching in a crawling position with hands and knees well spaced.

Some practice will be required in landing, so that hands and knees make contact with the bed at the same time. Although this is difficult, it is important, and must be perfected.

The trick is completed by pushing hard out of the bed with the hands and coming back onto the feet.

Hands and knees drop. (32.-35.)

32. Stretch up and push the feet gently backwards on take off.

33. and 34. Rotate to the hands and knees position, in the air.

35. Hands and knees drop landing position.

Front Drop

The front drop is another important basic exercise which forms the foundation for many other advanced stunts.

It is a quarter forward somersault ending in a landing on the entire length of the front of the body, and is then completed by rotating backwards to the feet. Some coaches prefer the performer to land on the front with the legs bent at the knees, as a preparation for an advanced trick called a Cody.

The correct landing position may be practised by lying on the floor, face downwards, legs together, either straight or bent at the knees and toes pointed. The face must be looking straight ahead, as if for the end of the trampoline, and the hands flat on the floor pointing towards one another and directly beneath the chin.

When the front drop is performed by an expert it will be noticed that:
1. He stretches straight and high at take off.
2. He drives his hips and legs backwards while lifting the top half of his body.
3. He drives his stomach downwards and effects a completely flat landing along the front of his body.
4. He focusses his eyes on the bed on the way down but does not drop his shoulders.
5. To complete the trick he pushes hard with his hands and rotates backwards to a standing position, having straightened his legs.

This is a complex skill to learn and must not be attempted before the pupil has perfected a good hands and knees drop. Even then the performer must learn this exercise through a series of progressions:
1. Practise the correct landing position on the trampoline bed.
2. Hands and knees drop.
3. Hands and knees drop, push the legs and hips backwards, flatten into front drop position.

Until stage three has been mastered stage four must not be attempted.
4. Front drop into a crash mat laid on the trampoline bed – from standing.
5. Front drop to trampoline bed from a low bounce.
6. Front drop to trampoline bed from a higher bounce, increasing height as the performer develops skill and confidence.

A common, serious fault is to dive into the landing position and land chest first, with the rest of the body following quickly. This is known as KABOOM, and can be quite dangerous. To rectify the fault the performer must learn to lift his shoulders, focussing his eyes on the end of the trampoline, and pushing his hips hard downwards.

The reverse of this is also common, with legs landing first and followed by chest and head, again causing KABOOM. The remedy for this is to lift high into the trick, and to drive the legs and hips hard backwards, and push the stomach down onto the bed.

This skill can be performed in three positions, tucked, piked and straight. The landing for each of these is the same but the flight positions are as the names imply.

The tariff value of this trick is 0.1 in each direction and therefore it is of little use competitively but it is of great value as a foundation for other tricks, particularly the forward somersault.

37

Front drop. (36.-39)

36. and 37. Stretch up and push the hips backwards to rotate into position.

38. Front drop posi-
tion in the air.

39. Front drop land-
ing position.

Back Drop

This exercise should not be learnt without the supervision of a coach.

This is a quarter back somersault which involves landing on the back then returning in a forwards direction to the feet. Since the take off for this trick is identical to that of the back somersault, it will be realised that the back drop must be learned properly.

When the back drop is performed by an expert, the following important points will be noticed:
1.   At take off he stretches his body straight and high.
2.   He lifts his chest and hips forwards and up. It must be remembered that the push of the hips should be gentle not vigorous.
3.   Throughout the trick the legs are kept straight particularly when landing.
4.   The performer makes contact with the bed with the whole of his back not just the shoulders.
5.   To complete the trick the performer pushes his legs up, looks for the end of the trampoline and returns to his feet.

Certain coaches advocate that the best landing position for the back drop is with the legs bent at the knees. The reason for this is to aid the kicking and beating action required to 'ball out'. We feel that this landing position is possibly dangerous for the beginner, since his legs may flick into his face on landing and injury might thus occur.

Learning the Back Drop
1.   When learning the back drop the performer should first practise the position shown in the photograph, either on the floor or by lying on the trampoline bed.
2.   The pupil should next slide a crash mat on the trampoline bed, and should get used to falling backwards onto the mat landing on his back.
3.   From a low bounce the performer should push his hips and feet forwards, at the same time locking his hips tight. From this position he should practise landing a completely flat back drop onto a crash mat.
4.   Next he should practise the push of the feet and hips, but pike into the landing position at the top of his bounce, and again land on a crash mat pushed onto the bed by two spotters while he was airborne.
5.   Once the coach is satisfied of the safety of the landing then the performer may attempt the exercise straight onto the bed, and regain the

40

standing position by lifting his shoulders forwards and up, and by pushing his feet in the same direction.

At no time must the performer allow his neck muscles to become loose, or kaboom may be experienced if his head flops back on landing.

Back drop. (40.-44.)

40. Stretch up straight and push hips and feet forwards for rotation. 41. Begin to pike into the landing position.

42. Piked in for landing.

43. Backdrop landing.

44. From landing push the hips and feet out and stretch up to feet.

Faults

These may occur with this skill if a performer drops his head and shoulders backwards at take off. This will cause the body to travel backwards. If this happens lift the head, shoulders, chest and hips forwards and up at take off.

This skill can be performed in three positions, tucked, piked, and straight. The landing for each of these is the same, but the flight positions are as the names imply.

The tariff value of the trick is 0.1 each way (to back drop – to feet), and is of value to competitors at grade three level. It is also of great value as a foundation for other more advanced skills.

Half Twist to Front Drop

This involves twisting in the air into a front drop position.

It is advisable to learn this move with the aid of a crash mat, since until the landing position is mastered the performer may experience violent kaboom. Before this move is attempted the pupil must be able to perform (a) half twist, (b) front drop.

The tariff value of this skill is 0.2 to front drop, and 0.1 back to feet.

Progressions

1. The performer should stretch up, lifting his chest upwards.
2. He should then stretch up and push his feet forwards.
3. As he pushes his feet forwards, he must look for the end of the trampoline. This will cause him to twist onto his front and land on the crash mat, provided by two spotters while he was airborne.

Half twist to front drop. (45.-47.)

45. Stretch up and twist from the bed.

4. Once the landing has been mastered the performer should attempt the skill on the trampoline bed.

5. The trick is completed by reverting to a standing position.

Kaboom may occur in the landing of this trick if the performer lands with his hips or chest first. Remedy – practise a good front drop and land it properly.

Faults

Twisting too early and not pushing the feet forwards at take off, casting to one side of the bed, or a kaboom landing are all common faults. Correct these by pushing the feet forwards at take off, and by looking at the end of the trampoline to which the feet are being pushed.

46. Half twist complete.

47. Front drop landing.

Half Twist to Back Drop

This move involves twisting in mid air and landing in a back drop position. It is executed from a good, high, straight bounce.

The tariff value of this skill is 0.2 to back, and 0.1 to feet. It is of value to competitors in grade three competitions, often forming the middle phase of tricks, such as the cradle (back drop, half twist to back drop) and the seat drop, half twist to back drop, so giving the added importance of being a basic twisting trick.

Only performers who can execute a back drop, front drop and half twist in safety should attempt this move.

Progressions

1. The pupil should perform a good front drop onto a crash mat, thrown onto the bed by the spotters, while he is airborne.

2. He should set up a good front drop and once he has gained this position in the air, his coach should call, 'Twist!' On this command the pupil should turn his head sharply and look for the ceiling, so causing his body to twist into the desired position.

3. Until the landing for this trick is mastered safely and regularly, the performer should land on a crash mat, not the bed.

Faults

The main fault which occurs with this move is that pupils twist too early and do not see the front drop position before the twist is executed. Early twisting causes all manner of problems on landing.

Half twist to back drop. (48.-50.)

48. Take off for a front drop.

49. Twist in the air.

50. Back drop landing.

Roller

The roller is described as 'seat drop, full twist around the length of the body to seat drop'.

Before the roller can be attempted safely the pupil must command the following skills:
1. Seat drop.
2. Front drop.
3. Full twist.

A good way of visualising the appearance of this skill is to imagine someone turning right over in bed. When the roller is performed by an expert the following important points will be noticed:
1. He performs the usual high, straight, bounce and as he begins to descend he gets into position for a good seat drop.
2. On take off from the seat drop position he extends his hips until his body is straight, (see photograph).

48

3.   As the hips are extended, he executes the twist by turning his head and shoulders in the direction in which he intends to rotate. It must be remembered that the twist is initiated from the bed.

4.   Having twisted through 360° he immediately lands in a good seat drop position.

5.   The exercise is completed by reverting back to a standing position.

  This trick must be learned through a series of steps.

(a)   The performer must first practise a seat drop, extending the hips until the body is straight in the air, then fall to seat drop.

(b)   Next he should learn to perform a seat drop , extending his hips and performing a half twist, landing on the bed in a front drop position. Until the front drop landing has been mastered the pupil may practise the landing on a crash mat, which two of the spotters may push onto the bed, while he is in the air.

(c)   The pupil must next execute the seat drop, half twist to front drop and from this position half twist out to seat drop.

(d)   Once stage (c) has been mastered the full trick may be attempted. All that is required to execute the full twist is that the performer looks in the direction in which he wants to twist, and follows his look with a twist of his shoulders.

Roller. (51.-55.)

51. Coming into a seat drop landing.

52. Seat drop landing.

53. Push the hips straight and start to twist.

54. Twist in the air.

55. Second seat drop landing.

Alternative Sequence

1.   The performer should lie along the red line on the trampoline bed on either his left or right side. If he lies on his left side he should prop his body up off the bed with his left arm thus:

2.   Assuming the performer to be on his left side he should now fire his right arm underneath his left arm pit. This will make him perform the full twist required for the roller. This process must be repeated a few times to condition his mind to the full twist.

3.   The performer should now execute a seat drop with hip extension back to seat drop, as in the first method stage (a).

4.   Next he may attempt the full trick. His training in twisting should enable him to accomplish the skill safely, if not perfectly.

Full Twist to Back Drop

The full twist to back drop is beautiful to watch, rewarding to perform and an important foundation for the full twisting backward somersault.

Its tariff value is 0.3 to back, and 0.1 to feet from back drop. This makes the exercise of value in grade three competitions.

As its name suggests, this skill involves a full twist around the longitudinal axis while rotating backwards to land on the back, finishing with the performer reverting to the standing position.

It will be noticed that when the full twist to back drop is performed by an expert:

1.   He lifts his chest up at take off.

2.   He pushes his feet forwards.

3.   As he pushes his feet forwards, straightens his body and locks his hips, he twists his head and looks for the bed, thus adopting a front drop position.

4.   Having seen the front drop position he turns his head again and looks

52

for the ceiling, so causing his body to twist into a back drop position and completing the full twist.

5.   Having landed the back drop successfully, he pushes his hips forwards, looks for the end of the trampoline and comes back to standing.

Progressions

The skill should be learned through the following sequence of events, and should be attempted only by performers who can execute front and back drops and half twist to back drop, safely and well.

1.   The pupil should perform a half twist to front drop, as described previously, and land it on a crash mat pushed onto the apparatus by two spotters while he is airborne.

2.   Next he should perform the half twist to front drop onto the bed, and immediately half twist out to a flat back drop position.

3.   Finally the pupil should attempt the complete exercise by performing a good high half twist to front drop, and after seeing the bed spin his head round to look for the ceiling, twist out onto his back and revert to standing.

   The skill must be learned with the aid of a crash mat and progressions must be strictly followed. The performer must not try to go on to the next stage until he has mastered each previous progression.

Full twist to back drop. (56.-60.)

56. Lift up and twist from the bed.

57. Quarter twist.

58. Half twist.

59. As the full twist is completed begin to pike.

60. Back drop landing.

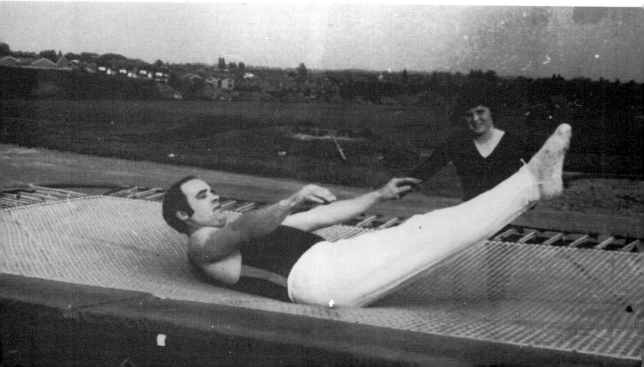

Back Drop to Front Drop

This involves landing a good back drop, and after rotating forwards through 180° and flattening out into a front drop landing, returning to the feet.

   The tariff value of this skill is complicated as the skill involves more than one contact with the bed. It may be expressed thus, 0.1 to back drop, 0.2 from back drop to front drop, and 0.1 to feet. This exercise involves three contacts with the bed and is therefore of little use as a competitive move. It is of great value however as a step towards learning more advanced skills e.g. to 'ball out'.

Progressions
Before attempting this skill a performer must be capable of executing a good back drop and front drop.

   The learning process should begin with the performer:

1.   Executing a good back drop with his legs straight and low.
2.   Next the pupil should repeat the back drop, and as he makes contact with the bed, gently beat his legs downwards, at the same time locking his hips tight and lifting his shoulders. This action will cause him to come quickly back to a standing position.
3.   After repeating stage two, again beating the legs downwards and this time rotating past the standing position, he then performs the front drop and lands into a crash mat, thrown onto the bed by two floor spotters, while the performer was airborne.
4.   After the front drop position has been landed successfully and regularly onto the crash mat, the exercise may be attempted onto the bed proper.

Faults
1.   Rotating from back drop to front drop can prove difficult if the legs are carried too high when landing the back drop. This means the beating action is difficult and there is a lack of rotation.
2.   Kaboom may be experienced when landing the front drop, and the causes of this are identical to those encountered in the plain front drop.
3.   Faults with the back drop landing will also be identical to those of the plain back drop.

Back drop to front drop. (61.-65.)

61. Back drop landing.

62. Beat legs through and lift up.

63. Start to look for the front drop.

64. Begin to descend for the front drop.

65. Front drop position in the air.

Front Drop to Back Drop

This is more difficult than the back to front drop but its tariff value is exactly the same.

It is of importance as a stage in the learning of a back Cody.

Performers intending to attempt this move must be able to perform a good front drop and back drop.

Progressions

1. A good front drop must be landed with the legs bent at the knees.
2. Stage one must be repeated but on landing the legs must be straightened sharply, this gives the body rotation and coupled with a push from the hands will bring the performer back to his feet.

The pupil must look at the end of the trampoline for as long as he can

Front drop to back drop. (66.-69.)

66. Front drop position with bent legs.

67. Kick the legs through to set up rotation.

68. Pike into the back drop position.

69. Back drop position.

during this exercise, and this will help him to lift his body upwards and prevent him from leaning backwards to gain rotation.

3.   Finally the performer must repeat stage two but rotate past the standing position and land a good back drop.

Faults

The main fault with this skill occurs when pupils land the front drop with straight legs, and are therefore unable to 'beat' to transfer rotation to the rest of the body. The transition from front drop to back drop is therefore awkward and usually performed in a tucked position.

The remedy is to land the front drop with bent legs and beat them straight on landing, the rest of the trick will then follow naturally.

Three Quarter Front Somersault

This is exactly what its name implies. It is a three quarter forward somersault which the performer lands on his back.

The tariff value of this trick is 0.3 and it is useful to performers in grade three competitions. It is of even greater value as a foundation for the crash dive and forward somersault.

Before a performer learns this skill he must be capable of performing a good hands and knees drop forward turn over to back.

When demonstrated by the expert, the pupil should notice the following points.

1.   At take off he lifts his head and chest up while looking at the end of the trampoline or the trampoline bed.

2.   At take off he pushes his hips backwards thus setting up forward rotation.

3.   As he rotates slowly over the top he watches the bed, and as he descends he pikes in, (ducks his head under) and sets up a back drop landing.

4.   Once he has landed in the back drop position, he pushes his feet forwards and up and looks for the end of the trampoline, reverting to a standing position.

Progressions

1.   Hands and knees drop, forward turn over to back drop.
2.   Full trick from standing into a crash mat thrown on by two spotters.
3.   Low bounce, full trick into crash mat until the landing is mastered.
4.   From normal bounce.

62

Three quarter front somersault. (70.-73.)

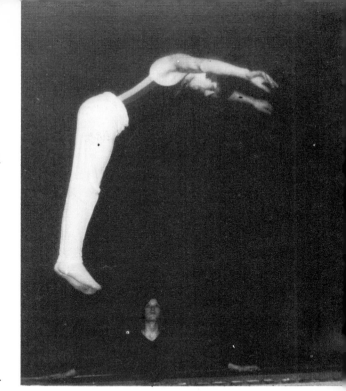

70. *(right)* Stretch up and push the hips and feet back.

71. *(below)* Start to pike under.

72. *(below right)* Pike in for a back drop landing.

73. Back drop landing.

Crash Dive

The crash dive is very closely related to the three quarter front somersault but is a rather more energetic affair.

Its tariff value is still 0.3 and this is the ideal trick from which to 'ball out'.

Any performer wishing to learn a crash dive must be able to perform a three quarter front somersault.

When performed by an expert the following points will be noticed in comparison with the three quarter front somersault:

1. At take off he reaches up with his arms, chest and head.
2. He drives his legs and feet hard backwards, locked at the hips in order to achieve a straight body position.
3. As in the three quarter forward somersault he watches the landing coming up and pikes in at the last minute to land in a back drop position.
4. After landing the back drop, he pushes his feet forwards and up, and looks for the end of the equipment and returns to a standing position.

Faults

The main faults with the three quarter front somersault and crash dive are fast, over rotation and slow, under rotation.

Fast, over rotation is caused by dropping the head and shoulders, which can be corrected by lifting them at take off. Under rotation is caused by insufficient drive from the hips or heels.

64

Crash dive. (74.-77.)

74. *(right)* Lift arms, head and chest up, driving hips and feet backwards.

75. *(below)* The top of the bounce.

76. *(below right)* Start to pike in.

77. Back drop landing.

Tucked Backward Somersault

This is generally accepted to be the least difficult of all somersaults because virtually throughout the trick the performer can see where he will land. For this reason it is usually the first somersault a performer learns.

The stunt itself involves rotating backwards for 360°, taking off from and landing in a standing position.

Before trying this skill a performer must be able to perform a good back drop without travel.

When it is demonstrated by an expert the pupil will look for the following points:
1. Before the trick is executed the performer stretches high, lifting his arms and chest as he takes off.
2. He drives his hips and feet forwards and up, thus causing his body to rotate backwards while keeping his head forwards and tucked in.
3. After driving the hips and feet he folds quickly into a tucked position bringing his knees up to his hands.
4. Almost as soon as his legs have passed over the top he 'steps out' of the tucked position ready to land on his feet.
5. The trick is completed by the performer landing on his feet on the same part of the bed which he used for take off.

Performers must not attempt to teach this move to themselves. A properly qualified coach will 'hand spot' the performer throughout each learn-

66

ing stage, and only when he is completely satisfied that the exercise is safe will the coach allow the performer to try the exercise unaided.

A coach will teach the performer the following progressions towards the backward somersault:

1. Take off position – the performer must be taught to stretch up.
2. Cultivation of rotation. The coach will hand spot this move so that the performer does not pass over the top until he is sure that the pupil has enough rotation to complete the somersault. Rotation is set up by the performer pushing his hips forwards at take off and flicking his straight legs towards the ceiling.
3. The rotation gained in stage two is speeded up by the performer tucking up after kicking.
4. As soon as the performer feels that he has passed over the top, he steps out and lands on his feet.

Many performers find that whilst learning the backward somersault they travel along the trampoline bed. This is a result of leaning and throwing the head and shoulders backwards at take off thus rendering the somersault dangerous. A conscious effort must be made to keep the head and shoulders forwards and tucked in so eliminating travel.

Do not attempt to teach this trick to yourself, your coach will be able to instruct you properly and catch you if you make a bad mistake.

Tucked backward somersault. (78.-83.)

78. Stretch up at take off.

67

79. The performer is beginning to tuck and is speeding up her somersault.

80. The tucked position. This is the fastest part of the somersault.

81. The performer steps out and looks for the end of the bed.

82. A check bounce landing completes the move.

69

Tucked Forward Somersault

This involves rotating in a tucked position through 360°. Both take off and landing are executed from feet to feet.

Contrary to popular belief, the forward somersault is more difficult than its backward counterpart because it is 'blind'. When performing it the pupil cannot see his landing position.

Performers should look for the following points when an expert demonstrates the forward somersault:
1. As with every exercise he stretches up high at take off and lifts his shoulders.
2. After take off he lifts his hips backwards and up, thus causing his body to rotate in a forwards direction.

70

3.   He snaps quickly into a tucked position and looks at his knees.
4.   As soon as his feet pass over the top he steps out of the tucked position, legs straight and ready to land on his feet.
5.   At landing, he looks for the end of the trampoline.
     Before a performer learns this trick he must be able to perform a good front drop and tucked jump.

Progressions

The advice and physical aid of the coach is of paramount importance to the performer who wishes to master this skill.
1.   This is usually the second somersault which a performer learns, and it is necessary to adjust his mind to accept a different direction of rotation. It is best done by asking the pupil to do some ordinary forward rolls along the bed.
2.   The pupil must speed up his forward roll and perform it with straight legs so eliminating the possibility of an errant knee breaking the performer's nose. The exercise is useful in helping the performer to learn rotation.
3.   Next the performer should learn to execute the good high tucked jump which forms the middle phase of the full somersault.
4.   Finally with the hand spotting aid of the coach the performer may attempt the full forward somersault, lifting his shoulders at take off, driving his hips backwards, tucking up, and as his feet pass over the top, stepping out and landing on his feet.
     Stage four will be learned while making the landing onto a crash mat slid onto the bed as the performer is airborne.
5.   The coach will discontinue support when he is convinced that the exercise is safe.

Faults

(a)   Performers often tend to travel along the bed in the direction of rotation – there are many reasons for this but the most common one is leaning forward into the trick. The pupil must always stretch up at take off.
(b)   Low fast somersault (dangerous) is caused by dropping the head and shoulders downwards at take off.
(c)   Falling over on landing – in the direction of rotation is caused by stepping out of the move too late.

Tucked forward somersault. (84.-87.)

71

84. Begin to stretch up at take off.

85. Lift up and drive the hips and feet into the somersault.

86. Tuck up tight, this speeds up the somersault.

87. An early step out to slow down the rotation and spot the landing.

Lazy Back Somersault

This is a three quarter back somersault which is landed in a front drop position. It is an exercise which must be learned under the supervision of a qualified coach.

Since this is a three quarter somersault its tariff value is 0.3. It is a useful competitive move because it finishes in the correct position to take off for a back Cody.

When performed by an expert, the pupil should look for the following points:
1. At take off the performer lifts his arms, head and chest, while still looking at the end of the trampoline.
2. He kicks his legs forwards, locks at the hips, keeping his body straight and rotates backwards.
3. As soon as his legs have passed the twelve o'clock position he looks for the cross on the centre of the trampoline.
4. Having seen the cross, he adjusts his body position to land a good front drop.

The most important part of this exercise is the landing, because unless the performer has the correct amount of rotation he will experience a kaboom action at touch down. As previously mentioned this can be both uncomfortable and dangerous. Coaches will hand spot this exercise and its progressions to ensure the pupil's safety while learning this skill.

Progressions
Before a performer learns this exercise he must be confident in performing both back somersaults and front drops.
1. The pupil should begin by performing a good back somersault.
2. He should then progress to back somersaults landed on hands and knees onto a crash mat. Here lifting and watching the bed should be emphasised.
3. The next stage is a back somersault to hands and knees unaided, again onto a crash mat which two spotters will have pushed under the airborne performer.
4. Once stage three has been mastered the pupil should execute a back somersault to hands and knees onto a crash mat and, from a hands and knees drop extend the body into a front drop and land it.
5. The final stage is to execute the full exercise repeatedly, developing good lift, flight and landings thus opening the door to a whole range of Cody somersaults.

88

Lazy back somersault. (88.-92.)

88. and 89. Stretch up with the arms, head and chest, also drive with the hips and feet.

89

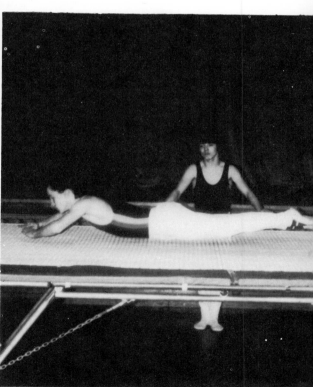

90. Start to look for the front drop position.

91. Front drop position in the air.

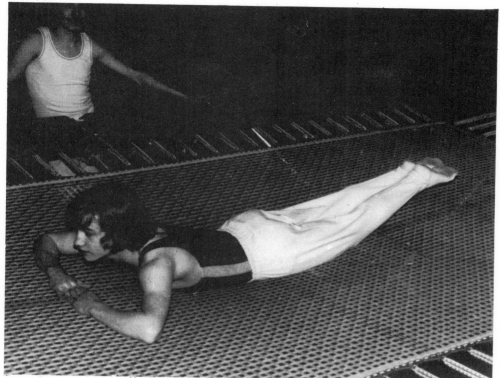

92. Front drop landing.

Barani

The Barani is a forward somersault with half twist. The tariff value of this skill is 0.5 and it is performed from feet to feet. This is the first twisting somersault which performers attempt, and it is important to them because it forms the foundation of many more advanced twisting somersaults such as Rudolphs and Randolphs. It can be performed tucked, piked, or straight which means that more than one type of Barani may be included in a routine without repetition. It is of value in grades three and two competitions.

When performed by an expert, a pupil will notice the following points about the piked Barani:

1. The performer stretches straight and drives his heels backwards at take off.
2. While stretching up and driving his heels and legs backwards, he locks at the hips and sets up forward rotation apparently around his shoulders.
3. He does not appear to twist until his feet have passed over the twelve o'clock position.
4. The performer watches the red line on the trampoline bed and twists by spinning his head round when he is completely upside down.
5. To complete the exercise he lands on his feet at the point on the bed which he used to take off.

Progressions

Before any pupil attempts a Barani he should be able to execute a good piked forward somersault and good half twist jump.

1. The performer must demonstrate the above skills to his coach so proving his eligibility to learn this exercise.
2. The coach will invariably hand spot this exercise making sure that the twist is timed properly and the landing is safe.
3. Supported thus the performer should set up his somersault and look for the bed at the appropriate moment. After much practice he will twist automatically at the correct time.
4. The performer continues to practise until his coach deems it fit for him to perform this skill unaided. A coach will always support or catch this skill until it is correct.

Under no circumstances should a performer attempt to teach himself this skill. It must be learned under the supervision of a qualified B.T.F. coach. If the Barani is learned and performed wrongly it may not only be hazardous to the performer but may inhibit the learning of subsequent twisting moves.

Faults

1. Early twisting converts a safe somersault into a dangerous side somersault. The remedy is to set up the forward rotation first – wait then twist.
2. Ducking the head and shoulders forwards and down at take off causes low, fast rotation and can be the cause of early twist and travel. The remedy is to stretch up at take off.
3. Always twist in the same direction as in other basic twisting skills.

78

Barani. (93.-97.)

93. Lift up and drive the hips and feet into a forwards somersault.

94. Start to turn the head for the twist.

95. Look hard for the end of the bed.

96. *(top right)* Twist complete. Look for the end of the bed and spot the landing.

97. Skill complete. Landing on the feet.

4. Competing

Man is instinctively competitive, and the arena of trampolining is as good a setting as any to exercise this instinct. Great fun can be gained from pitting your wits and skill against other performers, and in the process it is quite possible to learn a great deal about self discipline, balance and concentration.

Competitions may take all forms, from simple class affairs to organised county, regional, national or international matches. No matter at what level these occur, all who enter should go into the event with the will to win.

Competition Routines

Every performer in a competition must take part in two rounds. In each round he must perform a set of ten bounces in swing time – this is known as a routine.

The first round of any competition is known as the compulsory round, and here every performer attempts the same routine. This is to prove to the judges that the performer can conduct himself safely and correctly to the required standard. Marks are awarded for this routine as well as for the second round.

The voluntary routine usually follows after everyone has performed the compulsory, and here performers are allowed to demonstrate the spectacular side of their bouncing.

There are usually two or three grades of competitions. Grade three is the most basic form of competition; the requirements for this at regional level are that the performer should be able to perform forwards and backwards somersaults in ten bounce swing time routines. There should be no repeats of the same exercise in any routine.

81

Grade two is more advanced involving more twisting moves than in the previous grade, and grade one is the ultimate. This is obviously the standard of competition which all performers aim to reach. At this level of competition performers regularly perform double and even triple somersaults as well as multiple twisting somersaults in their routines.

Routines are given marks which are worked out by assessing the quality of each individual exercise. The judges are allowed to deduct up to 0.5 off each individual exercise in the routine. Voluntary routines are also awarded a mark for the degree of difficulty performed in each exercise. This figure is known as the tariff mark and is worked out as follows:
0.1 mark for every quarter somersault, so making any tucked somersault from feet to feet worth 0.4 mark.
0.1 mark is awarded for every half twist, so that a full twist jump is worth 0.2.

The position of the body during somersaults sometimes makes a difference to the total tariff value of the exercise, eg. single somersaults in the piked position are worth 0.5 because of the added difficulty of performing the somersault with straight legs, therefore the piked or straight body position on somersaults is worth an extra 0.1.

Where a move involves rotating around two axes, the tariff is worked out in this way:
Barani (Forward somersault with half twist).
  0.4 for forward somersault
  0.1 for half twist
total 0.5
Rudolph (Forward somersault with one and a half twists).
  0.4 for forward somersault
  0.3 for one and a half twists
total 0.7
Note– in twisting somersaults performers do not get an extra 0.1 if performed in a straight position.

The Planning of Routines

When planning a routine it is essential to take many points into consideration, for example suitable exercises for a grade three schools competition might be:

1. Seat drop.
2. Half twist to seat drop (Swivel hips).
3. Half twist to feet.
4. Piked straddle jump.
5. Full twist jump.
6. Tucked jump.
7. Back drop.
8. Half twist to feet.
9. Backward somersault.
10. Forward somersault.

When ordered properly these exercises would make an admirable routine, but as the order stands the routine would look unbalanced and probably feel very awkward to perform. Points which must be taken into account when planning a routine should involve the following:

1. Whether the moves lead naturally into one another. A good example of exercises which follow each other well could be Barani followed by back somersault. The landing of the Barani lifts naturally into a backwards motion, and thus sets up momentum for the backward somersault. It would be difficult to execute a forward somersault and then a backward somersault because the landing of the front somersault is blind, and the direction of the second exercise is completely opposite to the forward somersault. Plan routines so that they flow naturally – they will be easier to perform and look more impressive.

2. When planning a routine it is important to remember to put a simple exercise after a more difficult one in order to allow the performer time to balance himself, and maintain height and control throughout.

3. Never include exercises which cannot be executed safely or properly.

4. It is important to remember that if a routine is too demanding the performer will probably lose more marks for the lack of quality in his performance than the tariff mark awarded for the degree of difficulty performed.

5. Routines consist of ten contacts on the trampoline bed.

6. All routines must end with an exercise which lands on the feet.

So taking these considerations into account, probably the best arrangement for the routine listed earlier is:

1.	Backward somersault (tucked).	0.4
2.	Seat drop.	0.0
3.	Half twist to seat drop.	0.1
4.	Half twist to feet.	0.1
5.	Piked straddle jump.	0.0
6.	Back drop (piked).	0.1
7.	Half twist to feet.	0.2
8.	Full twist jump.	0.2
9.	Tucked jump.	0.0
10.	Forward somersault.	0.4
		total 1.5

Class Competitions

Knockout competitions provide an interesting break from teaching, and act as a useful stimulus to pupils to end the lesson on a high note and consequently work harder – after all who likes to be beaten!

These may take the form of 'Follow My Leader' where the coach performs an exercise or sequence of exercises, and each member of the group repeats the sequence. Additions may be made or a new sequence established at the beginning of each round.

'Add One' is another good game where each performer performs the exercises which have gone previously and adds his own exercise. This way a ten bounce routine may be quickly built up as performers get onto the trampoline for their turn.

The rules for these games are up to the individual coach.

Synchronised Bouncing

This is a very demanding form of competition and is the one true team event in the sport of trampolining. The object is for two or more performers to work on separate trampolines performing exactly the same routine at exactly the same time! This is not easy as the reader will appreciate.

It will be realised that if the team loses synchronisation, or if one or more of the performers fails to complete a routine, marks will be deducted. This is an exciting form of competition, and when there are large numbers of well drilled competitors it is a sight to behold.

General Advice

1. Never become conceited about your own performance and indulge in including exercises in your routine which you cannot perform safely. Be honest with yourself!
2. Out bounces. These are free bounces performed at the end of a routine which show the judges that a routine is complete and provide a polished finish.

We strongly advise the exclusion of these bounces unless the performer is extremely competent and experienced, since the judges are empowered to deduct further marks for poorly executed out bounces, despite the fact that the routine is complete.
3. Do not argue with the judges – there is an impartial referee who will air your grievances for you.
4. Prepare yourself thoroughly for routines and concentrate hard before you begin.
5. You may bounce as many times as you like to get yourself balanced before you begin your routine. Once started you may not stop and begin again.

Routines with their Tariff Values

Seat drop	0.0	Seat drop	0.0
Half twist to feet	0.1	Swivel hips	0.1
Pike jump	0.0	Half twist to feet	0.1
Half twist	0.1	Straddle jump	0.0
Straddle jump	0.0	Full pirouette	0.2
Back drop	0.1	Pike jump	0.0
Half twist to feet	0.2	Back drop	0.1
Tuck jump	0.0	Half twist to feet	0.2
Front drop	0.1	Tuck jump	0.0
To feet	0.1	Half twist	0.1
	0.7		**0.8**

Back somersault (free)	0.4	Back somersault (free)	0.4
Full pirouette	0.2	Seat drop	0.0
Seat drop	0.0	Swivel hips	0.1
Swivel hips	0.1	Half twist to feet	0.1
Half twist to feet	0.1	Pike jump	0.0
Pike jump	0.0	Back drop	0.1
Back drop (straight legs)	0.1	Half twist to feet	0.2
Half twist to feet	0.2	Full pirouette	0.2
Tuck jump	0.0	Tuck jump	0.0
Front somersault (free)	0.4	Front somersault (free)	0.4
	1.5		**1.5**

Back somie (straight)	0.5	Back somie (piked)	0.5
Pike straddle jump	0.0	Barani (straight legs)	0.5
Back somie (piked)	0.5	Back somie (tucked)	0.4
Tuck jump	0.0	Back somie to seat (tucked)	0.4
Back somie to seat (tucked)	0.4	Swivel hips	0.1
Swivel hips	0.1	Half twist to feet	0.1
Half twist to feet	0.1	Piked straddle jump	0.0
Piked jump	0.0	Back somie (straight)	0.5
Back somie (tucked)	0.4	Piked jump	0.0
Barani (straight legs)	0.5	Front somie (piked)	0.5
	2.5		**3.0**

The word 'free', in brackets after a move means a choice of tucked, piked or straight positions.

Analysis of Exercises

Trick	Fault	Reason	Solution
Swivel hips	Legs not passing underneath the body but going round the side.	1. Not enough lift.	1. Performer should lift arms, head and chest up.
		2. Twisting too early.	2. Look at end of trampoline as long as possible before twisting.
		3. Not looking at end of trampoline long enough when lifting out of first seat drop.	3. Return to seat drop half twist to stand, so the performer can feel the legs coming through, not round the side.
	Second seat drop landing, body drops down towards legs.	1. Result of twisting too early.	1. Look at end of trampoline as long as possible before twisting.
		2. Not leaning slightly back on second seat drop.	2. Performer should lean slightly back on second seat drop. Sit performer in seat drop position so he can feel how far to lean.
	Casting trick to one side when twisting.	Result of twisting too early, causing legs to go round the side.	Look at end of trampoline as long as possible before twisting. Stretch arms, head and chest up.

Trick	Fault	Reason	Solution
Front drop	Landing too high on chest.	1. Dropping head and shoulders into trick. 2. Diving into trick. 3. Pushing hips back too hard.	1. Lift arms, head and chest up, looking at end of bed throughout. 2. Lift arms, head and chest up, push hips back. 3. Reduce the effort from the hips.
	Landing on thighs causing kaboom to chest.	Lack of rotation due to the hips not being pushed back hard enough.	Push hips back at take off.
	Head dropping down to bed on landing, causing face to make contact.	1. Not looking at the end of trampoline. 2. Incorrect hand position.	1. Look at end of trampoline all the way through the trick. 2. Lay the performer in front drop position, and show him the hand position.
	Unable to rotate back to feet from the front drop position.	1. Pushing hips up first. 2. Not beating legs.	1. Lift head and shoulders. Look at end of trampoline. 2. Show performer bent leg landing position. Make performer beat legs hard.
	Falling backwards when landing on feet at the end of the trick.	1. Over rotation due to beating legs too hard. 2. Throwing arms behind the body when leaving front drop position.	1. Reduce effort when beating legs. 2. Stretch arms up.

Trick	Fault	Reason	Solution
Tucked backward somersault	Excessive travel.	1. Dropping head and shoulders back at take off. 2. Leaning back at take off.	1. Lift arms, head and chest up and forward at take off.
	Falling backwards on landing.	Over rotation due to: 1. Dropping head and shoulders into trick. 2. Driving hips and feet too hard. 3. Staying tucked too long.	1. Lift arms, head and chest up. 2. Reduce effort slightly from hips and legs. 3. Phase trick, tuck at top of bounce, then step out quickly.
	Gaining somersault too much.	Excessive push of hips, and dropping head and shoulders.	Lift arms, head and chest up. Reduce effort from hips. Drive feet into trick.
	Slow, under rotated somersault.	1. Not enough drive of the hips and feet. 2. Not tucking tight enough. Probably unable to tuck tight, because of action reaction due to head being dropped back at take off.	1. Drive hips and legs harder into trick. 2. Lift arms, head and chest up at take off.
	Twisting in trick.	1. Dropping one shoulder at take off. 2. Throwing one arm out sideways. 3. Looking round sideways when rotating in somersault.	1. Lift arms, head and chest up at take off. 2. Look at the end of the trampoline all the way through the trick.

Trick	Fault	Reason	Solution
Back drop	Landing too high on the back.	1. Dropping head and shoulders into trick. 2. Kicking legs too hard at take off. 3. Pushing hips too hard at take off.	1. Lift arms, head and chest up at take off. Give the performer's eyes a focal point. 2. Reduce effort from the legs. 3. Reduce effort from hips.
	Landing too low on the back.	Lack of rotation due to the lack of effort from hip push.	Lift chest, push hips up and forward.
	Kaboom from back to legs to back.	1. Landing too low on the back. 2. Trying to get back to feet still piked. 3. Legs too low and relaxed on landing.	1. Lift arms, head and chest up, at the same time push hips up and forward. 2. Push hips out from back drop position. 3. Lift leg position slightly. Give the performer's eyes a focal point.
	Falling forward after landing on feet at end of trick.	Generally this is caused by the performer's legs beating down from the back drop position causing a 'ball out' action.	Tell the performer to push his hips forward.

Trick	Fault	Reason	Solution
Tucked forward somersault	Excess travel.	1. Diving into trick by dropping head and shoulders.	1. Lift arms, head and chest up at take off.
	Fast and over rotation.	1. Dropping head and shoulders down at take off. 2. Tucking too early and staying tucked too long.	1. Lift arms, head and chest up at take off. 2. Phase trick, tuck at top of bounce then step out of tuck quickly.
	Falling backwards on landing.	1. Under rotation due to not enough drive from the hips and feet.	1. Drive hips and feet back into the trick. Lift arms, head and chest up at take off.
	Twisting in trick.	1. Dropping one shoulder at take off. 2. Throwing one arm out sideways. 3. Looking round sideways when rotating in somersault.	1. Lift arms, head and chest up at take off. 2. Look for the end of trampoline, to spot the landing position as soon as possible.

Trick	Fault	Reason	Solution
Barani	Excess travel.	Diving forward into trick.	Lift arms, head and chest up at take off.
	Fast, over rotation.	1. Dropping head and shoulders down at take off. 2. Twisting too late.	1. Lift arms, head and chest up at take off. 2. Twist when absolutely upside down.
	Falling forward on landing.	1. Not enough drive of the hips and feet at take off. 2. Twisting too early.	1. Drive hips and feet hard into trick, (don't drop head and shoulders because of the extra drive from hips and feet). 2. Twist when absolutely upside down.
	Side somersaulting.	Twisting too early.	Leave twist later.
	Casting to one side.	Twisting too early.	Leave twist later.

5.   Conclusion

It will be seen then that trampolining is a sport from which people of most ages can gain fun, excitement and a sense of achievement.

As an aid to bodily fitness the trampoline can rarely be surpassed. As newcomers to the sport will confirm, three minutes of hard bouncing are capable of reducing a seemingly fit body to a shadow of its former self.

While it will be seen that this piece of equipment is a source of fun and thrills, it will also be appreciated that any sport which involves being thrown into the air, rotating through at least 360° and often twisting as well, is a sport which must be treated seriously, and safety must be of paramount importance. Consequently we would repeat the following points:

1.   Do not become over confident, and do not show off.
2.   Always listen to your B.T.F coach's advice and act upon it.
3.   Do not fall into the trap of being tempted to ignore learning progressions. Follow them strictly and do not progress to the next stage before each previous stage has been mastered.

Many local education authorities offer evening classes in trampolining as part of their adult education schemes. Most secondary schools also offer trampolining lessons as part of their P.E. curriculum, and there is therefore every hope that this sport will soon be at the forefront of popular fitness schemes.

Britain has its own national organisation which is dedicated to the furthering of this sport – this is the:
British Trampolining Federation.
This organisation is responsible for arranging personal advancement courses, coaching courses, and competitions. It also provides newsletters, and seeks to further thinking and trampolining progress by gathering new ideas and publishing them for all serious trampoliners to see and discuss.

Additional information about this splendidly conscientious and thorough organisation may be obtained from the:

The British Trampolining Federation,
152a College Road,
Harrow,
Middlesex, HA1 1VH.
Telephone 01-863-7278

This book is intended as a source of reference and encouragement, not as an instruction manual. The methods and techniques expressed here are merely those which we have found to be effective, and must not be considered to have the force of law. Other coaches may have other methods which are equally safe and effective.

Finally we must express our thanks to the following people:
Derek Walters, Steve Blackmore, Tracey Green and Elaine Johnson for spending valuable time and patience performing for the photographs, and to Pete Leadbeater for his skill in photography.

We are grateful for the advice and guidance of John Duffy, B.T.F. Senior Advanced Coach.

Be safe and enjoy your trampolining!

The Language of Trampolining

In common with many other sports, trampolining has its own dictionary of words which coaches and performers alike use to describe stunts, techniques and faults.

For the benefit of newcomers to this sport, here are a few of the terms which are in common use.

BABY FLIFFUS. Ball out incorporating an early half twist.

BACK PULL OVER. A three quarter back somersault landing on the feet, having started from a back drop position.

BALL OUT. A one and a quarter forward somersault performed from either a back drop or crash dive take off.

BARANI. This is a forward somersault with half twist. It was named after an Italian acrobat who was reputed to have been the inventor of the move.

CAST. This is sideways movement across the trampoline bed.

CAT TWIST. Back drop, full twist to back drop.

CHECK BOUNCE. The action of stopping the bounce of the bed by bending the knees on landing.

CODY. This is a one and a quarter somersault in either direction forwards or backwards. (The back Cody is usually performed after a lazy back somersault from a front drop landing).

CORKSCREW. This trick is very busy! A back drop, one and a half twists to back drop.

CRADLE. The performer does a back drop, half twist to back drop. The twist may be early or late.

CRASH DIVE. A three quarter front somersault with the body in a straight position. The performer lands on his back.

FLIFFUS. Perhaps the strangest of trampolining terms. This is any double somersault, with twist.

GAIN. This is contrary motion along the bed to the direction of the somersault, e.g. forward movement in a backward somersault.

HALF TURNTABLE. A front drop, half twist to front drop.

KABOOM. This is a somersaulting action created by one part of the body landing after another. It is used particularly in the starting of a back Cody from a lazy back landing.

KILL. This is the act of stopping the action of the bed immediately on landing. If a coach yells 'Kill', at any performer, he will have good reason and the pupil must act on his word immediately.

KIP. Coaches often use the technique of depressing the bed with their own feet, as the performer lands, in order to give the pupil more height to do his trick. This is kipping.

LAYOUT. An absolutely straight body position, usually reserved for somersaults.

LAZY BACK. The performer executes a three quarter back somersault and lands on his front.

OUT BOUNCE. This is a free bounce which shows the judges in a competition that the routine is complete.

OVER THROW. Where a somersaulting performer passes his landing point and rotates past his feet, and for example lands on his chest by mistake.

PHASE. This describes the different parts which go to make up a trick. For example the three phases which go to make up a back somersault are, 1. take off, 2. tuck, 3. landing.

PIKED. Where the body is bent at the hips only.

RANDOLPH. A forward somersault with two and a half twists, and often known as a Randy.

ROLLER. Seat drop, full twist to seat drop. (Rather like turning over in bed).

ROUTINES. These are series of tricks; normally ten strung together in swing time, for use in competitions.

RUDOLPH. This is often called a Rudi. It is basically a forward somersault with one and a half twists.

SOMIE. Many coaches refer to somersaults affectionately as somies. If a teacher names a particular somersault, he may say – front somie, or back somie.

SPOTTER. A performer or spectator who guards the sides of the equipment to prevent injury to a performer through falling off the trampoline.

SWING TIME. This is the action of stringing tricks together, one bounce after another.

SWIVEL HIPS. A very stylish and simple move, which is a seat drop, half twist to seat drop.

TRAVEL. This is simply movement along the bed in the direction of rotation, eg. backward movement along the bed in a backward somersault.

TRICK (or SKILL). This means a trampolining manoeuvre. Other words which mean the same, are stunt, move and exercise.

TUCKED. The position of the body folded up tight at the knees and hips, with the hands grasping the knees.

TURNTABLE. A front drop with full twist around the lateral axis to front drop.